THE BACKYARD DETECTIVE

A GUIDE FOR BEGINNING NATURALISTS

BY DR. HERBERT H. WONG

ILLUSTRATED BY DEBORAH GREER

NatureVision™

Publisher's Cataloging-in-Publication Data
Wong, Herbert H.
   The Backyard Detective : a guide for beginning naturalists / by Herbert H. Wong ; illustrations by Deborah Greer.
   p. cm.
   Summary : Introductory guide for children to explore nature in their own neighborhoods. Includes nature activities, basic science classification, and journal writing.
1. Nature study–Juvenile literature.
2. Natural History–Juvenile literature. I. Title.
508-dc20   92-63342
ISBN 1-882489-00-4

NatureVision™
One Waters Park Drive, Suite 101
San Mateo, CA 94403

A portion of the profits will be donated to environmental education.

Manufactured in the United States of America
Printed on Recycled Paper

CONTENTS

PREFACE 4

WHAT IS A BEGINNING NATURALIST? 5

BACKYARD DETECTIVES BEGIN 6

    You're Equipped 9

    Backyard Detective Rules 16

BEGINNING TO EXPLORE: KINGDOMS 17

FUNGI, BACTERIA, AND ALGAE KINGDOMS 18

THE PLANT KINGDOM 19

    Non-Flowering Plants 19

    Flowering Plants 20

    Trees 22

THE ANIMAL KINGDOM 31

ANIMALS WITHOUT BACKBONES 32

    Insects 32

    Arachnids: Spiders......................................39

    Mollusks: Snails and Slugs 40

    Crustaceans: Pillbugs and Sowbugs 42

    Millipedes and Centipedes 43

    Earthworms 44

    Identify Your Creature 46

ANIMALS WITH BACKBONES 48

    Amphibians 48

    Reptiles 50

    Birds 51

    Mammals 54

KEEP UP THE GOOD WORK 56

JOURNAL 57

PREFACE

The Backyard Detective is a first guide to the environment for children ages five and up. It invites children to study nature by direct observation in easily accessible environments. With this guide as an outdoor companion, children use simple science tools and basic comparison charts to uncover their own areas of interest.

Diversity, interrelationships, adaptation, and change are the ecological concepts that form the framework for The Backyard Detective. These concepts are introduced to children in an informal style that encourages them to enjoy and respect their natural environment.

This guide is dedicated to all of Earth's children, young and old, whose natural curiosity and environmental consciousness deserve to be nurtured or respectfully reawakened.

Special acknowledgements to Kate McCormick and Liz Tsuji for their helpful assistance and persistent encouragement in bringing this project to reality.

HHW

To Backyard Detectives:

WHAT IS A BEGINNING NATURALIST?

A NATURALIST is someone who observes plants and animals where they live and studies how they interact with each other. You can become a beginning naturalist as you explore nature right in your own neighborhood.

Have fun with your science tools examining, digging, identifying, feeding, growing, measuring, writing, drawing, tracking and collecting clues! Enjoy creating your first nature journal.

The Backyard Detective helps you find the clues around you. Make up your own questions about what you see and try to find the answers. Then you will know that you are on your way to becoming a lifetime naturalist!

BACKYARD DETECTIVES BEGIN

Backyards, frontyards, schoolyards and gardens are all natural discovery places. They are close to home yet full of things to explore. Rocks and paths, plants and animals, even puddles of water have stories to share and mysteries to solve.

Once you begin to follow clues, you can watch plants and animals change and grow. Some, like snails and slugs, pave their own roads as they travel. Others jump, hop, fly, swing, climb, hang, and slide. How do they do it? Who are all these busy neighbors of yours?

By following along in this guide, you will get to know them better—trees, flowers, mammals, birds, reptiles, insects, and amphibians.

TAKE A CLOSER LOOK!

Your adventures as a Backyard Detective begin when you pick a spot outside to investigate. Even a small area has lots of clues because it can be the home for many plants and animals.

The natural home of a plant or animal is called a HABITAT. Some insects live their whole lives on one plant. Other animals, such as squirrels, have much larger habitats, which may include many backyards and frontyards. Habitats can be on the ground and even in the ground.

Woodpiles, tree stumps, dead leaf piles, rotting logs, flower pots, bricks, rocks and fences all hold surprises and lots of evidence. Animals hide under these places to keep cool and damp.

As weather changes, habitats change, and you will find new clues to investigate. You can keep exploring your spot at different times of the year, and even at night, to see how it changes. You can also pick different areas in the same yard and compare what you find in each place.

YOU'RE EQUIPPED!

As a Backyard Detective, you are already equipped with your own senses to help you explore and make discoveries.

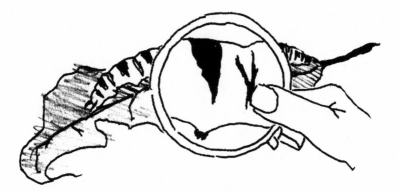

PEEK AND STARE

Your EYES can see things close up or far away. Peeking and staring at plants and animals is fun. Look at clues like colors, sizes, shapes, patterns and markings.

SHHH...LISTEN!

Your EARS can hear all kinds of sounds in nature. Sounds have shapes, sizes, shades and patterns. They can be short or long, low or high, smooth or wavy, sweet or sour. Listen for a buzz, a hum, a rattle, a screech or a whistle.

Songbirds are great singers who make wonderful music. Listen for the sounds of rain-drops, crickets, tree frogs, or humming-birds. Stop and listen: what sounds do you hear now?

Robin

SNIFF, SNIFF!

Your NOSE helps you to sniff and smell. Different flowers and leaves give off smells or odors. GET CLOSE AND SNIFF!

Skunks and stinkbugs are easy to identify by smell. Do you know others? Even damp soil has a smell. Start sniffing!

TOUCH AND FEEL!

Your HANDS can give you clues by touching and feeling. Touch a variety of plants. Separate hairy and furry ones from the smooth or rough ones. Compare the feel of a dry fallen leaf with one that is living.

Gently touch a pillbug with your finger and see why it has its name. Or touch the feelers of a snail or the big foot of a slug. What happens? How do your fingers feel?

Touching a Pillbug

MORE DETECTING TOOLS

There are a few other things a Backyard Detective will find helpful when investigating:

1.   A MAGNIFYING LENS is a great tool for exploring. You can see things close-up. Use it often to stare at tiny creatures and plant parts.

2.   Use a small PLASTIC JAR to examine small creatures. It must have holes in the lid for animals to breathe. The jar is really a temporary home. Return your animal to where you first found it so it will be free again in its own habitat.

3.   The PENCIL you use to make notes in your journal is also handy for turning over wood or stones when you look for insects. Make sure you put everything back in the same place you first found it.

4.   With a MEASURING TAPE you will be able to measure the size of your plants and animals and distances between things and places.

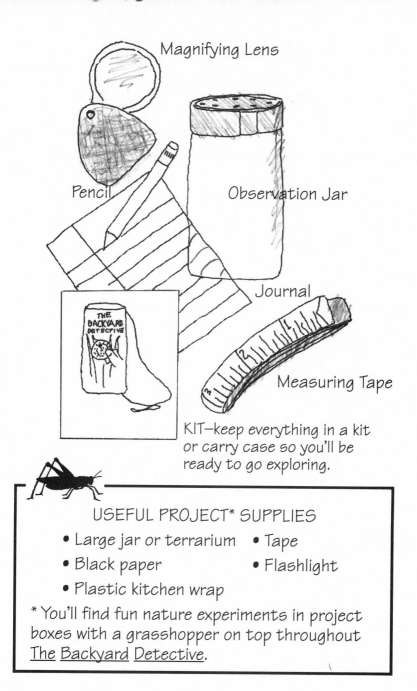

Magnifying Lens

Pencil

Observation Jar

Journal

Measuring Tape

KIT—keep everything in a kit or carry case so you'll be ready to go exploring.

USEFUL PROJECT* SUPPLIES

- Large jar or terrarium
- Tape
- Black paper
- Flashlight
- Plastic kitchen wrap

* You'll find fun nature experiments in project boxes with a grasshopper on top throughout <u>The</u> <u>Backyard</u> <u>Detective</u>.

Date/ Time	Notes (Place, Weather, Observations)
May 3 2:00pm	I saw a robin eat a wiggling worm.
	This book has special pages for
	your journal writing. Please turn
	to Page 57 to begin keeping a
	record.
	Do it now!

5. Keep a record in your JOURNAL. When you explore, it is easy to forget some of the things that happen. Write about what you see, hear, find, or wonder about. Make drawings to help you remember what you see. You can also ask an older friend for help.

Here are tips on taking notes in your journal:

- WHEN does it take place? List the date, time of day, and the weather. Is it a cool or warm day? Is it sunny or cloudy, windy or calm?

- Tell WHAT the animals are doing. Are they hunting for food, eating, resting, hiding or sleeping? Tell how they move from one place to another.

- You can COMPARE the size of all kinds of clues. Use your measuring tape to record distances and sizes. Measure the length of animal tracks or around a tree trunk.

- ADD anything interesting you see. Be sure to draw pictures or take photos. You will be glad you did!

BACKYARD DETECTIVE RULES

1.   The first rule of nature exploration is to look for clues. LOOK, LISTEN AND TOUCH, BUT DON'T DESTROY. A Backyard Detective can uncover nature's evidence and still leave the scene so others can enjoy it.

2.   HOW TO TREAT YOUR EVIDENCE

- DO make NOTES in your journal.

- DO RESPECT all living things. Don't take plants or animals out of their habitats without permission. Some living things are scarce. You may scoop an insect into your jar to study or keep it for a short while. Always return it to the spot where you found it.

- BE CAREFUL! A few creatures can be dangerous.   A female black widow spider should not be touched. It is a large black spider with a red mark on its belly. (See drawing on Page 39).

- LEAVES OF THREE—LET ME BE! Look out for leaves that are grouped in threes. They may be poison oak or poison ivy, and can make you itchy!

Poison Oak

THE FIVE KINGDOMS: BEGINNING TO EXPLORE

When you go outside, you see that the natural world is bustling with many kinds of living things. To help you learn more about them, here are some words scientists use to organize and describe them.

A living thing is called an ORGANISM. There are many kinds of organisms, and scientists long ago divided them into groups.

The largest groupings are called KINGDOMS. Two of the largest kingdoms are plants and animals. Organisms from most of the kingdoms live together right in your backyard. Some you can see and some are too small to see even with your magnifying lens.

THE FIVE KINGDOMS OF LIVING CREATURES

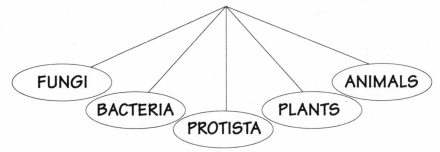

FUNGI   BACTERIA   PROTISTA   PLANTS   ANIMALS

FUNGI, BACTERIA and ALGAE KINGDOMS

Mushrooms and toadstools belong to the FUNGI KINGDOM, and so do lichen that grow on rocks and trees. Be careful: some mushrooms are poisonous. Draw a picture of the mushroom shapes you find. Be sure to include their colors and where you see them.

The BACTERIA KINGDOM includes small organisms that cannot be seen without a microscope. They live almost everywhere. Some kinds of bacteria are helpful, such as soil bacteria that break down dead plants into soil and others that help to make yogurt and cheese. "Germs" is the name for harmful bacteria that can cause illness.

Algae and seaweed remind us of plants, but they belong in their own PROTISTA KINGDOM because they are different inside from plants. Algae and seaweed both need a watery habitat to live.

THE PLANT KINGDOM

When Backyard Detectives pick places to investigate, the first things they notice might be trees, shrubs, and flowering plants.

NON-FLOWERING PLANTS

The plant kingdom is made up of plants that have flowers, and some plants, such as mosses and ferns, that do not grow flowers. Mosses are tiny plants that grow in cushion-like clumps in damp, shady places. They can hold large quantities of water until they need it. Look for moss growing on tree branches and rocks in shady spots.

Ferns are other plants that do not grow flowers. Their large green fronds grow from small fuzzy balls. See if you can find a fern and tell the difference between new growth and fully grown fronds.

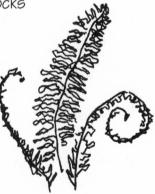

While you are looking at the fronds, see if there are any small dark spots called SPORES on their undersides. They are part of the fern's life cycle to grow new ferns.

FLOWERING PLANTS

Whether the spot you investigate is dry or damp, hot or cold, you will find many types of flowering plants. They include trees, flowers, grasses, vegetables, and shrubs. They all have leaves and roots and special pathways in their stems and trunks to carry water and other food through the plant.

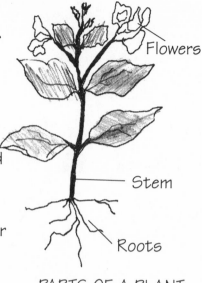

PARTS OF A PLANT

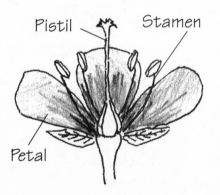

PARTS OF A FLOWER

They give us fruits, vegetables, cool shade, beautiful colors and fresh flower smells. Plants clean the air for us. Some provide the wood for our homes. What are some of the other things they give us?

Flowers are the way most plants make seeds which grow into new plants. Sometimes you can see seeds growing as flower petals wilt. If you have a fruit tree nearby, you can watch the flowers change into seeds or fruit as the seasons change. Look at a rosebush to see if you find any seed pods. They grow round and hard at the base where the flower was. How many kinds of seeds can you find? What plants do they come from?

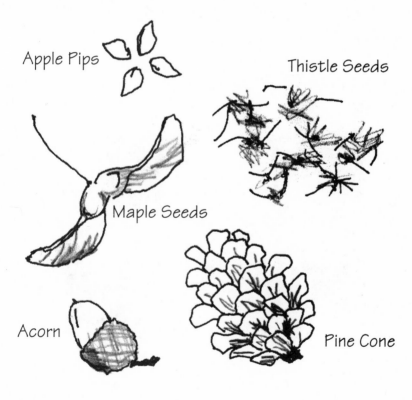

Apple Pips

Thistle Seeds

Maple Seeds

Acorn

Pine Cone

TREES

When do you call a plant a tree? A tree is woody and tall and lives a long time.

Trees are some of the biggest living things. The tallest living trees are redwoods that live along the coasts of California and Oregon.

You can study trees month by month through the seasons. Watch for changes and record them in your journal. Trees have different shapes, bark, and leaves.

BARK

Smooth

Ridged

Scaly

Peeling

NEEDLES AND LEAVES

A tree with cones is usually a pine, spruce, fir or one of their relatives. These trees are called EVERGREENS. Can you guess why? Many people know the Monterey Pine. It is found in parks and lots of gardens. It has leaves with two needles in a bundle. How many evergreen trees can you see today? What kind of needles does each have?

Most trees with broad flat leaves are called DECIDUOUS. They lose all of their leaves in autumn. You may know a maple or oak tree. Look at a leaf for its arrangement and shape! Is there one leaf growing on each stem or is there more than one?

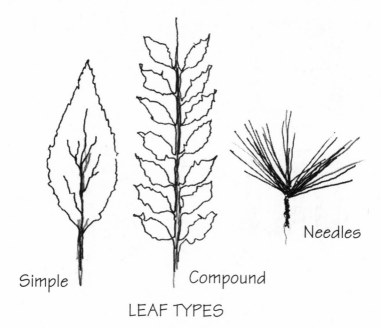

Simple   Compound   Needles

LEAF TYPES

LEAFY THINGS TO TRY

LEAF PRINTS ARE FUN!

It's fun to make leaf prints by tracing them in your journal. You can also make colorful prints of different leaf shapes with crayon or paint.

LEAF SAMPLES

Collect green leaves in the spring in your journal. Tape or glue the leaves with rubber cement onto each sheet. Write where you find each one and the name of the leaf if you learn what it is. Measure your leaves to find which is the largest and which is the smallest. Make room for a sample of the leaf in the fall season to show changes. To keep the leaves clean, you can use plastic wrap pressed down closely on the leaves.

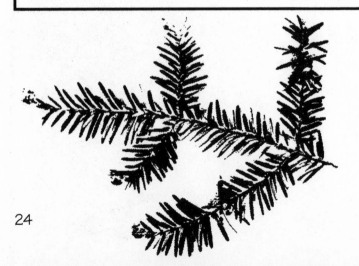

LEAF WATCH

Stand under a tree and watch the leaves drop in the autumn months. Can you hear a leaf fall from a tree? Try counting the number of leaves that fall in three minutes to get an idea of how fast they fall.

CAN YOU SMELL IT?

Trees such as cottonwood, birch, and black walnut have twigs and leaves with odors or smells of their own. Crush their leaves and sniff. Describe what they smell like. Record what you think each smell reminds you of. Can the bark of a tree smell like a pencil? Get up close to the bark of a cedar tree and sniff hard. Many pencils are made of cedar wood.

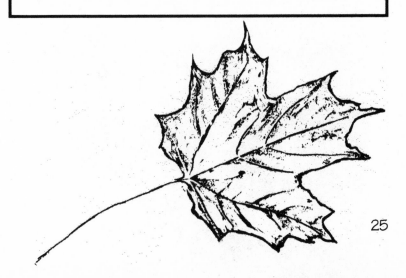

NATURE'S APARTMENT BUILDING

NATURE'S APARTMENT BUILDING

A tree is like nature's apartment building from its tip to its roots. A great community of plants and animals lives in different layers and parts of the tree. Notice that even dead trees are homes to many plants and animals.

PLANTS MAKE A YARD MORE LIVELY!

You can plant trees and flowers to make your backyard more attractive to birds and butterflies. Brightly colored flowers are very inviting. Birds love to eat the fruit of berry bushes. Look in your yard: do birds have a favorite spot? Do you see a sheltered area where you could make a special place for birds with their own pool and snack bar? What a great project for your family or classroom.

White Breasted Nuthatch

ADOPT A TREE

You can adopt a tree that you like a lot and make it your special tree. Keep track of your tree through Spring, Summer, Fall and Winter with an all-year calendar. Describe your tree's habitat and what happens from its top to its bottom. Write a tree biography or life story in your journal.

Find out as much as you can:

1. Measure how big around it is with a measuring tape.

2. Take photos of the tree or draw close-ups of its bark, leaves, buds, fruit and other parts that you see throughout the year. Keep notes and pictures in your journal.

3. Make a survey of what animals do in and around the tree. What animals make it their home? Do they find their food in the tree or somewhere nearby? See which birds nest there and in what parts of the tree. Keep track of the eggs and later, the baby birds. How long do they stay in the tree?

4. What birds feed on the top of the tree? Can you find clues of a woodpecker at work? Listen for its hammering on bark. Many insect-eating birds feed at different levels and places on a tree. A creeper climbs up the bark hunting for insects in the cracks. It uses its sharp beak to dig out food. You might see birds like chickadees or warblers busy filling their tummies with goodies. Don't forget to watch for squirrels!

5. Check on the soil and leaves piled up at the bottom of the tree. Many tiny animals live in these habitats. Have your jar and magnifying lens ready!

THE ANIMAL KINGDOM

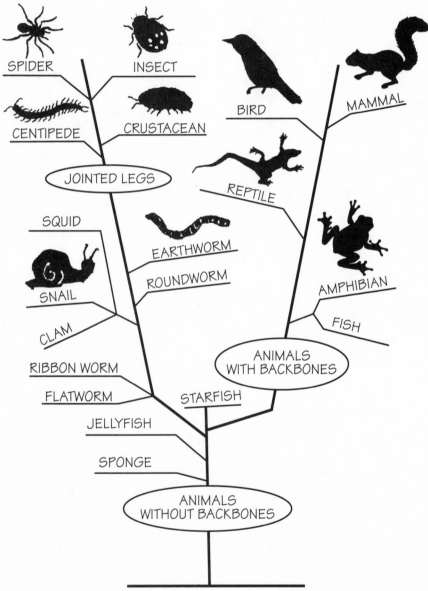

THE ANIMAL KINGDOM

Many kinds of animals live in backyards. They are as small as tiny mites and as big as birds and mammals. Even though they are very different, they ALL belong to the animal kingdom.

How are animals different than plants?

- Plants cannot move about, and animals can move by themselves.

- Plants make their own food with sunlight and water, but animals eat plants or other animals.

What other differences can you think of?

The Animal Kingdom includes animals <u>without</u> backbones and animals <u>with</u> backbones. There are many more animals without backbones than animals with backbones. Some animals without backbones are insects, spiders, worms, snails, and sowbugs. Some animals with backbones that you might find in your yard are birds, rabbits, gophers, and squirrels.

ANIMALS WITHOUT BACKBONES

INSECTS

LADYBUGS AND APHIDS

Let's start with your magnifying lens and jar. Look for insects feeding on plants. What you find depends on the kinds of plants growing in your yard. Look around rosebushes for ladybugs and aphids.

Ladybugs are red, orange or yellow with black spots. Some do not have spots at all. They eat aphids, sometimes called plant lice. Aphids suck juices from plants for food. Which are easier to see on green rosebush leaves, ladybugs or aphids? Why?

Ladybug

A ladybug is a beetle, a kind of insect. Look at the three main body parts, six legs and two feelers. It has four wings. The two soft ones are its flying wings, and they are covered by the colorful hard wings. Watch how a ladybug folds its dark flying wings after landing.

Drop rosebush leaves with lots of aphids into your jar. Watch out for the sharp thorns. Find ladybugs nearby and gently touch one in your hand. Sometimes it will turn over and pretend it's not alive! Put the ladybugs in the jar and watch them feed on aphids. See what parts they don't eat!

Look for tiny yellow eggs on the leaves. Put some of them in the jar, too. Keep them in your jar and see what happens in about three weeks. Watch for funny looking insects without wings that come out of the eggs. They are called larvae and will grow up to be ladybugs. Write about your ladybugs in your journal.

Remember to let them all out of the jar when you finish watching them.

ANTS! ANTS! ANTS!

Each animal finds its own food and living space. Most small animals live in or on the ground in cool, damp, dark habitats. Look under rocks or rotting logs. What are some of the animals hiding in these places?

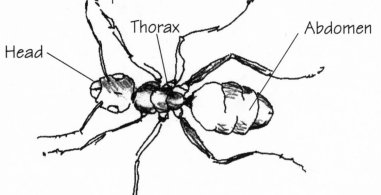

Thorax

Abdomen

Head

Ants are no strangers. These insects are active and easy to find. Ants come in different kinds, sizes and colors. The ones nearby may be worker ants searching for food. The same kinds of ants live together in colonies or nests. They dig out tunnels and large rooms in the ground and in rotting logs. These are nurseries to bring up young ants and to store food.

Can you spot an ant that is bigger than the other ants? It's a queen ant. It can lay thousands and thousands of eggs.

To collect some ants, use a small paintbrush to brush them onto a plastic spoon. Put the ants into a plastic bag and tie it tightly. You may also collect small white ant eggs, ant cocoons and small wiggly larvae. Put the bag in the refrigerator for an hour to slow down the ants. Brush them into your large jar half filled with soil.

Cover the outside of the jar with black paper. In about an hour when you take off the paper to peek, you'll see ants building tunnels next to the glass. Your magnifying lens will bring them up close. How many legs can you count? See the big eyes and jaws. An ant's head is connected to its chest by a very short neck. A thin waist connects its chest and stomach.

Add a few drops of water to keep the soil damp. Feed ants some cereal, fruit, bread crumbs and some sugary water or honey. Record the foods they eat in your journal. Put the ants back in your yard so they can make new nests.

BUTTERFLIES AND MOTHS

Butterflies and moths are insects that are colorful flyers. They may seem to be alike, but you will find some differences in the Butterfly/Moth Chart. It will also help you to find them at different stages of their lives.

	BUTTERFLY	MOTH
BODY	SLENDER	HEAVY SET
WING POSITION	LIFTED	FLAT
ANTENNAE	KNOBBED	FEATHERY
ACTIVE PERIOD	MOSTLY DURING THE DAY	MOSTLY NIGHT
PUPA	CHRYSALIS (NO COCOON)	PUPA IN COCOON

A caterpillar is one stage in the life of a butterfly or moth. Caterpillars are easy to keep and observe. They eat the leaves of the plants where you find them. Put a caterpillar and the leaves it's eating in a large jar. Make sure it always has fresh food. Measure the length of your caterpillar. Which will yours become, a butterfly or a moth?

DEVELOPMENT OF THE
MONARCH BUTTERFLY

 Egg

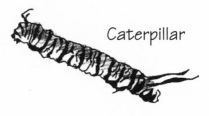 Caterpillar

 Chrysalis

Adult Butterfly

SUPER JUMPERS AND MUSIC MAKERS

Crickets and grasshoppers are fun to watch. They are great jumpers. Their large back legs are strong. Both crickets and grasshoppers are noisy insects.

You can find grasshoppers on a warm day where it is grassy by listening for their songs.

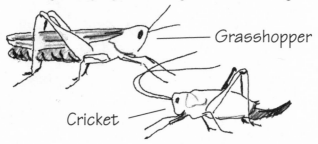

Grasshopper

Cricket

Crickets live in cracks in the ground and other shady places out of direct sunlight. They have short wings and can't fly so they move by jumping in the air. Only male crickets chirp.

Put moist sand at the bottom of your large jar with some leaves. Catch a cricket with a paper bag or net and watch it for a few days. Feed it bits of apple, lettuce, potato peelings, seeds or other scraps. Crickets eat almost any kind of food. How does your cricket use its jaws to chew?

A SPIDER ISN'T AN INSECT??

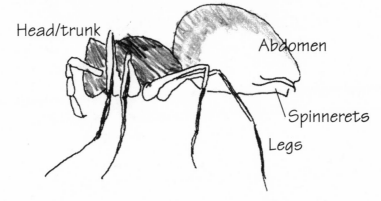

Head/trunk

Abdomen

Spinnerets

Legs

   A spider is in its own family called ARACHNID and has eight legs, not six like an insect. It has two main body parts, and an insect has three. Insects also have antennae, jaws, and wings, and spiders do not.

   Spiders do have SPINNERETS which allow them to spin webs of liquid silk. Each kind of spider spins its own kind of web. Some webs are even spun in the ground. How many kinds of webs can you find? Where did you find them?

Black Widow Spider

Sometimes spiders may look scary, but few can harm you. DO NOT TOUCH a female black widow spider. It is half an inch long with a red mark on its belly.

STALKING SNAILS AND SLUGS

Early in the morning in spring and summer, when the ground is still soft and damp, you can

Snail

creep up on snails and slugs. Look for them under fallen leaves where they hide to stay cool. They are active at night, too.

A good clue is the shiny, sticky trail they make. They move slowly on these smooth trails. Look for them on leaves, grass, rocks, flower pots and logs. Another clue is holes in leaves.

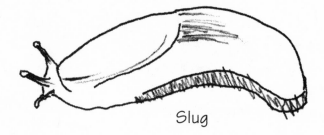

Slug

Snails and slugs are close relatives. They are related to clams and squid. They are all MOLLUSKS. Most mollusks have shells. A snail's shell grows as the snail grows. It can hide in its own shell, too!

Put one or two snails or slugs in your jar and watch one move across the jar. See how its large foot stretches out and holds onto the jar.

Snails and slugs eat the same plant foods. With your magnifying lens, look at one of their bodies through the jar to see the mouth. Watch one scrape food with its tongue. Look at the mouth! Watch them eat celery, carrot, apple and lettuce. They eat and eat!

They have four horns on their head that are like feelers. The two big ones have eyes. A shorter pair below are for touching and "smelling" things. Tap the side of the jar. What happens to the feelers?

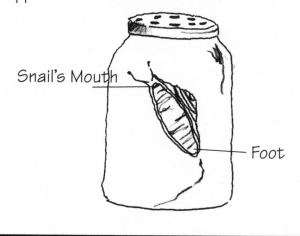

Snail's Mouth

Foot

PILLBUGS AND SOWBUGS

The outdoors are full of hiding places for wood lice. You know them better as sowbugs and pillbugs. They are NOT insects. They are relatives of shrimp and are all called CRUSTACEANS. Turn over bricks, rocks, and pots to find them. They hang onto the bottoms of things or squeeze under and between things.

Sowbug

Pillbugs curl up into tight round balls when they are bothered. Sowbugs flatten themselves to the ground to hide. They are all about the size of the fingernail of your second finger. Count the number of legs. Are there seven on each side?

Pillbugs and sowbugs can't live long in dry air. They dash for damp places! They have a hard shell on their backs like a coat of armor. It protects them from birds and spiders.

What kind of habitat do sowbugs and pillbugs like best? Put dry soil on one half of the bottom of your jar and moist soil on the other half. Drop a pillbug or sowbug into the jar and see what happens.

MILLIPEDES AND CENTIPEDES

Millipedes and centipedes look like worms. They are in their own family. How are they different from earthworms? For one thing, they have many legs, and earthworms have no legs. How are millipedes and centipedes different from each other?

Millipede

	MILLIPEDES	CENTIPEDES
NUMBER OF LEGS	100-200	ABOUT 30
NUMBER OF LEGS ON EACH PART	TWO PAIRS	ONE PAIR
MOVEMENT	GLIDES	WRIGGLES
FOOD	PLANT MATTER	INSECTS, WORMS & SLUGS
SAFETY TO YOU	SAFE TO TOUCH	MAY BITE – BE CAREFUL

Centipede

EARTHWORMS

Once you decide to investigate earthworms, you will find that they are easy to collect. They are very active at night. They come up from the soil to find leaves to eat. You can collect them or track them with a flashlight. Worms also come up when it rains so they won't drown.

During the day, you can find clues where earthworms live under the soil. You may find trails of dirt bumps left behind by earthworms who eat the soil when they tunnel through. These are called CASTINGS. Dig into the ground and search.

Use your magnifying lens to watch a worm stretch out and shorten its body to move. How long is it when it stretches out? How long is it when it's shortened?

Make a worm jar to see how earthworms tunnel through soil. Fill half of a large jar with soil. Collect four or five earthworms. Put them in the jar with leaves you find on the ground for food. Keep the jar in a cool spot at home or school. Sprinkle in a few drops of water to keep soil moist. Wrap dark paper around the jar to keep out sunlight. Take it off when you want to see the worms.

How do they move their bodies in the jar? What does a worm do when it gets to the top of the soil? Can you see them eat soil when they tunnel? Which end is the front end of the worm? Try tapping the table where your jar is sitting. What happens?

IDENTIFY YOUR CREATURE

	ANT	SPIDER	SNAIL
TYPE	INSECT	ARACHNID	MOLLUSK
HABITAT	IN THE GROUND AND ABOVE THE GROUND	IN THE GROUND AND ABOVE THE GROUND	DAMP, DARK PLACES
NUMBER OF BODY PARTS	3	2	HEAD, FOOT AND BODY SHELL
NUMBER OF LEGS	6	8	NO LEGS!
FOOD	PLANTS AND ANIMALS	MAINLY INSECTS	PLANTS

CHECK THIS CHART!

PILLBUG	MILLIPEDE	EARTHWORM
CRUSTACEAN	MILLIPEDE	SEGMENTED WORM
DAMP, DARK PLACES	DAMP, DARK PLACES	DIRT
14	DOZENS	100-180 DIVISIONS
14	TWO PAIRS FOR EACH DIVISION	NO LEGS!
PLANTS	PLANTS	SOIL AND PLANTS

ANIMALS WITH BACKBONES

AMPHIBIANS

Toads and frogs are both AMPHIBIANS, but they are different in many ways. Take a good look at the Toad and Frog Chart.

	TOADS	FROGS
HABITAT	SHADY, DAMP YARDS (AWAY FROM WATER)	MOSTLY PONDS AND STREAMS
BODY SHAPE	FAT	SKINNY
LEGS	SHORT FRONT & HIND (BACK) LEGS; GOOD FOR HOPPING	STRONG, LONG HIND LEGS; GOOD FOR LONG JUMPS
SKIN	DRY, ROUGH, WARTS	MOIST, SMOOTH, SOFT
BUSY TIME	DAY	NIGHT

Toad

Both toads and frogs are big eaters. Watch how a toad's long, sticky tongue darts out to catch a moving insect. Rarely will it eat anything that does not move. If a toad catches an earthworm that is too big, it will use its front feet to stuff the earthworm in its mouth. Then it swallows the worm in one big gulp!

Set up a moist toad habitat in a large jar or terrarium. Put some gravel or sand in the bottom. Top it with damp soil. Put in a few plants from shady places in the garden. Set a little plastic container of water into the soil. Toads like to soak in water. Make sure the jar cover has holes. You'll find your toad in a shady area. Feed the toad some worms and watch it catch them to eat.

Do you see the toad stick out its tongue when it eats? Does it blink its eyes?

Frog

SALAMANDERS

Related to toads, salamanders also live in shady, damp places under dead leaves, rocks and well-rotted wood.

Don't get salamanders mixed up with lizards. Salamanders have no claws or scales on their bodies, and they can't live in hot, dry habitats. They have smooth, moist skin. When you see something that looks like a big earthworm with four legs, you probably have found a slender salamander.

Keep a salamander in a large jar in a habitat such as the one you make for a toad. Just add a small piece of wood or a rock. Feed the salamander with caterpillars, ants, sowbugs or worms.

LIZARDS

Lizards are scaly animals. They are REPTILES like snakes and turtles. Lizards have four legs with five toes on each foot. The toes have claws. They live in dry, hot habitats. Their scaly skin helps to keep their body moist. Lizards are fast runners, not like their slow moving relative, the turtle.

Look for lizards on a warm, sunny day in your yard. They like to sit in the sun on rocks, sand and fences. Fence lizards often live in backyards.

A BIRD WATCH

Look for clues of bird life. Can you track down any feathers or nests? Maybe there's a nest in a tree or on a nearby roof. It should not take long for you to hear birds singing or calling to each other.

Birds are so active they need lots of energy to keep going. They spend most of their lives looking for food and eating. Robins, starlings, and waxwings have fruit in their diet. House sparrows, goldfinches, towhees, juncos, and house finches like seeds. Nuthatches, wrens, creepers, flycatchers, and woodpeckers eat many kinds of insects. Birds that eat insects move quickly through trees and shrubs.

Downy Woodpecker

You can use binoculars to see birds' beaks and feet better. Their beaks are designed for special jobs such as pecking, cracking, spearing or tearing. Their feet are designed to run, climb, or scratch.

PARTS OF A BIRD

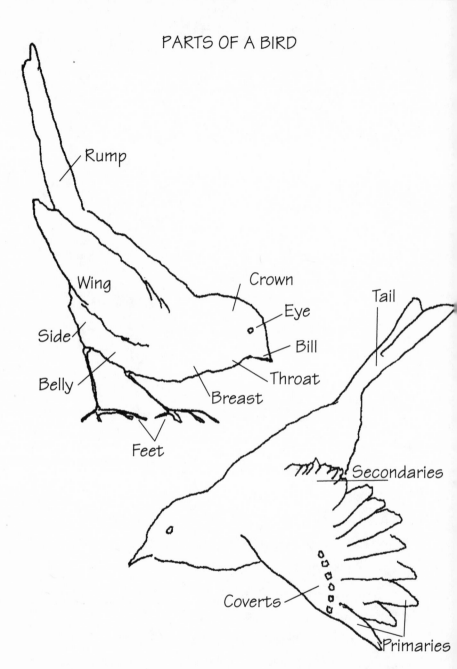

Rump

Wing

Crown

Eye

Side

Bill

Belly

Throat

Breast

Feet

Tail

Secondaries

Coverts

Primaries

FUN BIRD THINGS TO DO

Here are some things you can do to observe birds in your backyard.

1. Set up a bird feeder to attract birds for close-up looks. It can be as simple as hanging a milk carton with a hole cut into it. Put in a variety of bird seed. You can buy seed at pet and garden stores. Seed-eating birds will soon make your yard a regular stop.

2. Get a beginning bird book. Start a checklist of birds you see and note the date. Learn about bird shapes. What kind of beaks do birds have? Compare the different ways birds behave.

3. Listen to tapes of bird calls and songs. There are also videotapes of birds in their habitats.

A MAMMAL WATCH

Not very many mammals are active during the day. But squirrels are! In your yard notice how squirrels eat bird food from your bird feeder tray! Squirrels make nests of leaves on high tree branches or in tree holes. Look for them in the fall and winter when trees have dropped their leaves. They run on the ground, through trees and along telephone wires. Most of the time they are hunting for food.

You may get a peek at gophers and moles. Both of these mammals have underground homes. Look for signs such as mole hills on your lawn and flower beds. Check on the hills every week to see if anything changes. Moles hunt for worms that drop into holes in the ground.

For other mammal signs, see if tree bark has been ripped or torn from the trunk or branches. These are signs of mammals with claws. What could they be? Mice, skunks, raccoons and opossums are mammals of the night. Look for signs of their food search.

Meadow Mouse Tracks

The best clues and signs may be animal tracks. Follow the tracks for clues about mammal activity. Look at field guidebooks on animal tracks for help. Study the charts to match tracks with animals.

Raccoon Tracks

KEEP UP THE GOOD WORK!

The Backyard Detective is only the beginning of your nature exploration. You have made a great start investigating the clues in your own neighborhood. You can continue this adventure:

VISIT: Parks and nature preserves

Natural science museums

Environmental education centers

Zoos

Libraries

TALK TO: Local naturalists

Science educators

Librarians

READ: Nature books and magazines

JOIN: Nature and environmental education groups (e.g. The Audubon Society and National Wildlife Federation)

EXPLORE: NEW habitats. Your backyard detecting skills can be used everywhere.

Date/ Time	NATURE JOURNAL Notes (Place, Weather, Observations)

Date/ Time	Notes (Place, Weather, Observations)

Date/Time	Notes (Place, Weather, Observations)

Date/Time	Notes (Place, Weather, Observations)

Date/ Time	Notes (Place, Weather, Observations)
	61

Date/ Time	Notes (Place, Weather, Observations)
62	

Date/ Time	Notes (Place, Weather, Observations)
	63

Date/ Time	Notes (Place, Weather, Observations)